Contents

Any words appearing in the text in bold, **like this**, are explained in the glossary.

What are drugs?

A drug is any substance that affects your body and changes the way you feel. There are three groups of drugs – **medicines**, **legal drugs** and **illegal drugs**.

Medicines

Many medicines, such as cough medicines and painkillers, help to soothe the symptoms of a disease. Other medicines, such as antiseptic cream and antibiotics, tackle the disease itself. Some medicines can only be **prescribed** by doctors, but others can be bought from a chemist or from shops such as supermarkets.

Illegal or legal?

Legal drugs include medicines, of course, but the term usually refers to drugs such as alcohol and tobacco. These drugs affect the way a person feels but are not illegal for adults. Tea, coffee and cola are legal drugs too. Illegal drugs include cannabis, **heroin**, Ecstasy and **LSD**, and are forbidden by law.

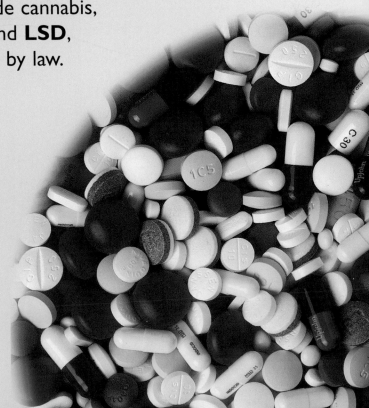

Medicines are often taken in the form of pills. It is important only to take pills that are prescribed for you and to follow the directions on the bottle or box.

Learn to Say No!

Cannabis

Angela Royston

Heinemann
LIBRARY

www.heinemann.co.uk
Visit our website to find out more information about **Heinemann Library** books.

To order:
 Phone 44 (0) 1865 888066
 Send a fax to 44 (0) 1865 314091
Visit the Heinemann Bookshop at www.heinemann.co.uk to browse our catalogue and order online.

First published in Great Britain by Heinemann Library,
Halley Court, Jordan Hill, Oxford OX2 8EJ
a division of Reed Educational and Professional Publishing Ltd.
Heinemann is a registered trademark of Reed Educational & Professional Publishing Ltd.

OXFORD MELBOURNE AUCKLAND
JOHANNESBURG BLANTYRE GABORONE
IBADAN PORTSMOUTH (NH) USA CHICAGO

Designed by AMR
Illustrations by Art Construction
Originated by Ambassador
Printed in Hong Kong/China

05 04 03 02 01
10 9 8 7 6 5 4 3 2 1

ISBN 0431 09905 7
This title is also available in a hardback library edition (ISBN 0 431 09900 6)

British Library Cataloguing in Publication Data
Royston, Angela
  Cannabis. – (Learn to say no)
  1.Cannabis – Juvenile literature 2.Cannabis – Physiological
  effect – Juvenile literature 3.Drug abuse – Juvenile
  literature
  I.Title
  362.2'95

Acknowledgements
The Publishers would like to thank the following for permission to reproduce photographs:
Chris Honeywell, p.15; Corbis, p.7, p.10 (Dan Lamont), p.11 (Galen Rowel), p.28 (Todd Gipsteir), p.29 (Owen Franken); Environmental Images, p.4 (Dave Ellison); Gareth Boden, pp. 22, 24, 26, 27; Image Bank, p.19 (Thierry Dosogne), p.21 (Peter Turner); Rex Features, pp.18, 20; Science Photo Library, p.6, p.8 (Mark De Fraeye), p.17 (Matt Meadows/Peter Arnold Inc.); Tony Stone, pp.5 (Simon Norfolk), p.23 (David Roth), p.25 (David Young Wolff); Topham Pictures, p. 9.

Cover photograph reproduced with permission of Eye Ubiquitous and Tony Stone

Every effort has been made to contact copyright holders of any material reproduced in this book. Any omissions will be rectified in subsequent printings if notice is given to the Publisher.

These are all illegal drugs which can be dangerous to take. They include stimulants and depressants (sometimes called **uppers** and **downers**) and hallucinogens.

Uppers and downers

Apart from medicines, most drugs are **stimulants**, **depressants** or **hallucinogens**. A stimulant, such as caffeine, makes the body work faster. A depressant, such as alcohol, slows the body down and makes the person relax. A hallucinogen alters the way a person sees or hears things. Cannabis is both a depressant and a hallucinogen. This book tells you about cannabis, what happens when people use it and the dangers it brings.

Did you know?

There are many different slang words for cannabis and people are always making up new names for it. Names for cannabis include dope, tea, pot, soap, blow, hash, ganja, **grass**, dagga, kif, weed, wacky backy and draw.

What is cannabis?

Cannabis is made from a plant whose proper name is *Cannabis sativa*. There are four forms of the drug cannabis and each has a different name – **hashish**, **marijuana**, sinsemilla and cannabis oil.

Hashish and marijuana

Hashish, or hash, is a hard, brownish-black block. It is made by drying the whole plant and then rubbing it to make the **resin** into hashish. Some hashish is stronger than other hashish, depending mainly on where the plant was grown. Marijuana, also called **grass** or weed, is not as strong as hashish. It is made from the green leaves and stalks, which are dried and chopped. Hashish and grass are the most common forms of cannabis.

Sinsemilla and cannabis oil

Sinsemilla is made from the male flowers of the plant and is stronger than most forms of hash. Cannabis oil is made from the juice. There is debate as to whether it should be allowed to be legally **prescribed** as a medicine for **multiple sclerosis** and other diseases. It is also given to lessen the unpleasant side effects of **chemotherapy**.

Cannabis is a kind of **hemp** and grows easily in most parts of the world. Every part of the plant can be made into the drug.

These special pipes are called hash pipes. Hash or grass is placed in the bowl and smoked. Most people, however, roll the drugs up with tobacco to make a joint.

How cannabis is used

Cannabis is usually smoked but it can also be cooked or made in the same way as tea, with boiling water. Grass and hash are usually mixed with tobacco and rolled into a **joint** or smoked in a pipe. Grass is sometimes smoked without tobacco to make a very strong joint.

Did you know?

Cannabis contains more than 400 different chemicals. When it is smoked it produces over 2000 chemicals which are breathed into the lungs. Many of these chemicals damage the lungs and other parts of the body.

Which is true?

It is said that during the Crusades Muslim fighters used to be given hashish before being sent off to kill Christians. Today people say the opposite – that cannabis makes people feel relaxed and more sympathetic to those around them. Do you think that both views could be true, depending on the circumstances?

A mixed history

People have been using cannabis for thousands of years. They used it not only for pleasure, but as a medicine. A Chinese book of remedies collected for Emperor Shen Nung included it nearly 5000 years ago. The drug then spread to India and by the 1840s doctors in the West began to use it too. In England, Queen Victoria's favourite doctor treated many illnesses and complaints with cannabis.

Chinese medicines use many kinds of herbs, and other things such as sliced horn. The herbs are weighed and put into plastic bags, ready for use.

An illegal drug
In Britain the government passed laws in 1928 making it illegal to use cannabis for non-medical purposes, although at the time few people were using it anyway. Nine years later the United States government made possessing or selling cannabis a crime.

Increasing popularity
In spite of these laws, the drug became very popular during the 1960s and 70s. Many young people in Europe, North America and Australia began to smoke cannabis regularly. It became the most commonly used **illegal drug**. In the 1970s a survey estimated that 43 million Americans (nearly 20% of the population) had tried cannabis.

The debate

In 1973 Britain banned its use as a medicine along with the use of other drugs like heroin. Since then many people have called for the ban to be lifted on cannabis, particularly for treating **cancer**, **multiple sclerosis** and other illnesses. Some people argue that cannabis is less harmful than alcohol and tobacco and that it should no longer be an illegal drug, but others argue that we need to know more about its harmful effects before the ban is lifted.

Did you know?

The Ancient Greeks used juice from cannabis seeds to help cure indigestion. In the late 1800s it was used as a remedy for coughs, rheumatism, asthma, migraines and period pain. Cannabis was not illegal then and so it could be bought and sold like other herbs and medicines.

In the 1960s many young people began to smoke cannabis, commonly known as **marijuana**. It became part of a 'hippie' way of life, which included a particular style of music and clothes.

Think about it

Many people who were hippies in the 1960s and 70s look back on that time as an exciting and idealistic age. Other people say that hippies only remember the good things and forget about the problems and difficulties. What do you think?

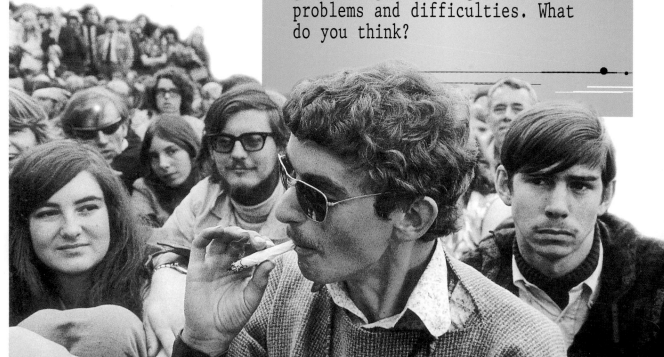

Cannabis and the law

Possession

Cannabis is an **illegal drug**. It is against the law to have it in your **possession**, for example in your pocket, among your belongings or at home. When people smoke cannabis they usually make a **joint** and pass it from one to the other, each taking a puff. Everyone who holds the joint is legally guilty of possession.

In some countries and states adults and older teenagers will probably not be taken to court for possessing a small amount of cannabis, but in Britain they would probably receive a **caution**. The caution is recorded on a national police computer and anyone who has been found with cannabis a maximum three times will then be prosecuted and go to court.

The police seize tonnes of drugs every year. About 80% is cannabis.

Drug dealing

Selling or supplying drugs is a much more serious offence. This is known as **drug dealing**. Dealing includes giving cannabis to others, even as a gift. If someone is caught with a large quantity of cannabis, the police assume that they are a dealer and will arrest them, particularly if the cannabis is divided into several smaller amounts.

Smuggling drugs is a very serious offence. This specially trained sniffer dog can smell drugs on people and in luggage.

In Britain the penalty for dealing in cannabis is up to five years in prison or a fine, or both. The situation in other countries varies. In the Netherlands, for example, the police usually do not arrest people for smoking small amounts of cannabis in special cafés. In many countries, like Thailand, however, the penalties for possessing and dealing in cannabis can be very severe.

Cannabis cafés

Some cafés in the Netherlands sell cannabis openly. Smoking cannabis is not legal there but the police do not usually prosecute, although some cafés have been closed down due to problems with more dangerous drugs. What do you think are the advantages of not prosecuting cannabis users?

Did you know?

In Britain in 1995, 40,000 people were cautioned for unlawfully possessing cannabis and 24,000 were **prosecuted**. Of those prosecuted, 13,000 were fined and 930 were given a prison sentence. In the same year, 4600 people were prosecuted for dealing and nearly 700 of them were imprisoned.

What happens when cannabis is smoked?

Lung damage

When someone smokes cannabis the smoke goes down their windpipe and into their lungs. The smoke from cannabis is very hot and burns the throat and damages the delicate lining of the lungs. Some people hold the smoke in their mouth to let it cool before breathing it in. In the lungs, **chemicals** from the cannabis and from any tobacco used in the **joint** pass into the blood and are pumped all around the body.

Poisonous chemicals

The main chemical in cannabis is Tetrahydrocannabinols, called **THC**. However, cannabis also contains many of the chemicals present in tobacco, but in a more concentrated form. Cannabis contains more **tar** than tobacco. Tar collects in the lungs and can cause **cancer**. Cannabis, like tobacco, contains hydrogen cyanide (a deadly poison), ammonia and carbon monoxide. Carbon monoxide reduces the amount of oxygen in the blood and damages the heart. Joints that are mixed with tobacco also contain nicotine, a very **addictive** chemical.

Smoking cannabis begins to affect the body after a few minutes and lasts from 3 to 5 hours. These are some of the physical effects.

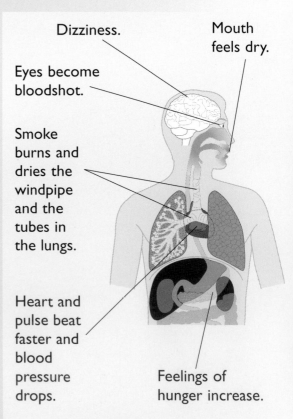

Dizziness.

Mouth feels dry.

Eyes become bloodshot.

Smoke burns and dries the windpipe and the tubes in the lungs.

Heart and pulse beat faster and blood pressure drops.

Feelings of hunger increase.

Eating cannabis

When cannabis is cooked and eaten, the drug passes through the stomach and is digested into the blood. It begins to effect the body about an hour after it is swallowed. Eating cannabis may avoid the hazards of smoking, but the main problem is that it is harder to control the amount taken. Once swallowed, it cannot be **diluted**.

Varying strengths

Hashish contains about five to eight times the amount of THC as **marijuana**. **Skunk weed** is also much stronger than other kinds of marijuana. Joints also vary in strength, depending on how much cannabis is used. Since cannabis is an **illegal drug**, its sale is not regulated and the drug may be mixed with other substances. There is no way of knowing how strong or how pure it is.

Did you know?

Cannabis is a form of **hemp**, a plant which is made into rope, twine, canvas and clothes. Hemp is produced in many countries in the world, including the United States, but cannabis is grown mainly in parts of North Africa, the Near East and southern Asia. It is also grown by people for their own use in Britain and other countries.

A cigarette made with cannabis is called a joint. A joint contains up to 3 times as much tar as a cigarette. It also contains more cancer-causing chemicals.

An average cigarette contains about 15mg of tar.

A joint gives up to 3 times as much tar as a cigarette because it is packed more loosely and doesn't have a filter. Users also hold the smoke in their lungs for longer which leaves 40% more tar.

13

The effects of smoking cannabis

The effects of cannabis are not very obvious, particularly at first. A person may smoke several times before they notice any effect at all. Even then, they may only notice that they are talking and laughing a lot, but not realize that it is due to the cannabis.

Stoned

A person is said to be '**stoned**' when they are clearly affected by cannabis. They will be more aware of sounds and other sensations. Some people become talkative, while others become lethargic and withdrawn.

Some people feel particularly 'in tune' with what they are doing. They may feel that they are playing their guitar unusually well, for example. In fact, people who are stoned perform less well at all tasks. The illusion of performing well is particularly dangerous for anyone who is driving a car. Cannabis affects judgement and co-ordination, both of which are very important when driving.

Think about it

Cannabis affects a person's sense of time, memory, balance and co-ordination. What sort of problems could these lead to? Imagine, for example, if someone walked home after a party before the effects of cannabis had worn off.

Depression and anxiety

Cannabis can cause many unpleasant feelings. A person's experience of cannabis will be affected by their mood. Some people may feel relaxed and sympathetic to people around them. But if they are depressed, cannabis can make them more depressed. Some people become anxious and may panic, particularly if they are not used to the drug. If a lot of cannabis is taken, the person loses track of time and may become forgetful and confused. Since their balance and co-ordination are affected, people who are stoned are more likely to have accidents.

Cannabis makes colours more intense and shapes sharper. In the 1960s patterns like this were called 'psychedelic' and were often designed by people who liked the effects of cannabis and LSD.

Frequent use and its effects

Effects on the body

Cannabis is not physically **addictive**. This means that although people may smoke it regularly and heavily, their body does not need it to function normally. Unlike an alcoholic, who has to drink increasing amounts to get drunk, a cannabis user does not need to smoke more to become **stoned**.

However, cannabis is harmful to the body. Cannabis contains many **chemicals** that cause **cancer** of the lungs, the throat and the neck. Tobacco also contains cancer-causing chemicals, and it is thought that cannabis may increase the deadly effects of tobacco. Cannabis increases the problems of people with heart disease, such as hypertension and hardening of the arteries.

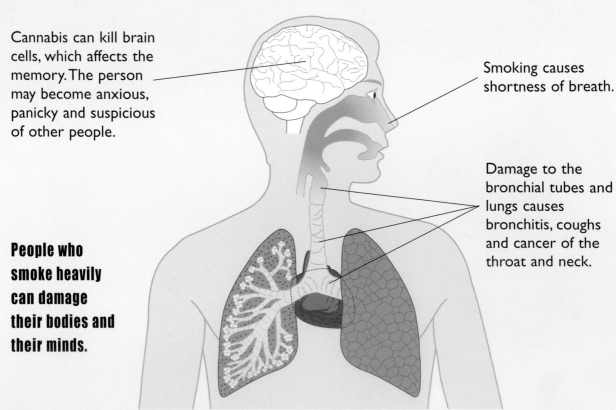

Cannabis can kill brain cells, which affects the memory. The person may become anxious, panicky and suspicious of other people.

Smoking causes shortness of breath.

Damage to the bronchial tubes and lungs causes bronchitis, coughs and cancer of the throat and neck.

People who smoke heavily can damage their bodies and their minds.

16

Unborn babies

Pregnant women who regularly smoke a lot of cannabis may affect their babies. When the mother takes cannabis into her body some of it passes through to her unborn baby. For several months after it is born the cannabis in the baby's body may cause it to shake, be easily startled and distressed. Babies whose mothers regularly use a lot of cannabis are more likely to be born **prematurely**.

Did you know?

If someone smokes heavily, for example several times a week, the drug can stay in the body for up to a month after the last time they smoked.

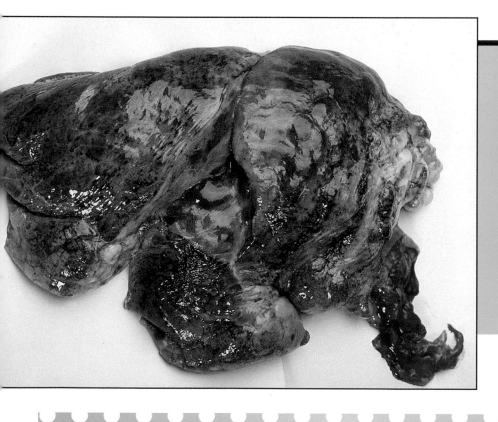

Cannabis is often mixed with tobacco when it is smoked. Cannabis and tobacco both damage lungs and can cause diseases such as lung cancer. These are the lungs of a smoker; they are dirty and damaged.

Assessing research

Scientists do not agree on how harmful cannabis is. Some studies say that it damages the brain and the body's ability to fight disease. Other studies have found no evidence of damage and even claim that it helps the body fight disease. Why do you think different studies might arrive at different results?

The social effects

Addiction

Cannabis is not physically **addictive** but it can be psychologically addictive. This means that some people rely on it to feel happy and sociable. The effects of a **joint** can last for several hours, so by smoking two or three joints a day people can be **stoned** for most of the time. When they are not stoned, they may be very bad tempered and some people become **paranoid**.

Losing touch

Heavy smokers of cannabis lose their motivation. They tend to spend most of the time sitting around and not getting on with their lives. They may have big plans but they do not put them into action. Students may not work properly and may fail their exams. People who are stoned most of the time become cut off from their family and their work. They become isolated and lonely and this can make them smoke more.

Being stoned most of the time stops people living their lives. They may have big plans, but do nothing to put them into action.

18

Crime

Cannabis is not cheap so heavy smokers have to pay for it somehow. Some turn to crime such as stealing so that they can sell the stolen items for money. People who buy cannabis from **dealers** are in danger of getting involved in crime too. If they buy cannabis for their friends as well, and are caught, they will be accused of **drug dealing**. Dealers are criminals who may also deal in drugs such as **heroin**, **LSD** and other dangerous drugs. They often frighten their customers and try to make them buy other drugs. Some dealers let first time customers have the drugs supposedly free on approval. However, the dealers soon want their money. The users often can't afford to pay the dealers back and so turn to crime.

Most people who use heroin and other dangerous drugs began by smoking cannabis. But most cannabis-users do not go on to use other drugs.

Did you know?

A quarter of an ounce (7 grams) of cannabis costs about the same as two video-tapes or two CDs. For the price of half an ounce you could buy a new pair of trainers or other clothes.

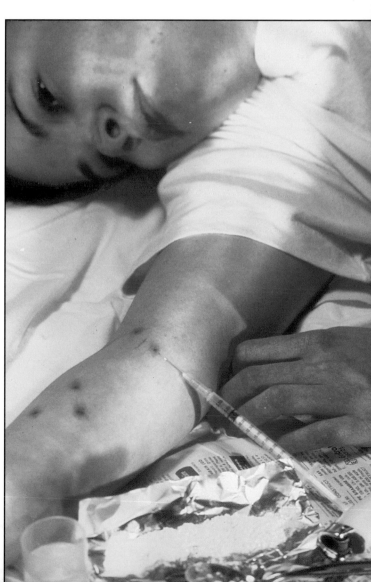

Why do some people do it?

Following the crowd?

Some people use cannabis because it helps them feel more confident and less shy. As **joints** are usually passed around, with each person taking one puff at a time, cannabis can give people a feeling of sharing and friendliness. But how real are these feelings? You should be able to be yourself and have good friends without cannabis.

Most people try cannabis because they are curious and because their friends are trying it. But it is important to do what you want and not just follow what other people do.

People often think that open-air festivals, such as Glastonbury, are a safe place to take drugs. But drugs are just as illegal inside a festival as they are outside of it.

Marijuana mystique

Cannabis is illegal and can be harmful. Some young people find it exciting to break the law and defy their parents and teachers by smoking it. It makes them feel independent and 'cool'.

Smoking cannabis gives people the feeling that they know about something that ordinary people don't know about. Others try to show how 'cool' they are by talking about how **stoned** they have been. But don't believe everything that people say about being stoned. Some people exaggerate the effects because they do not want to admit that they did not feel anything very much.

Cannabis has a strong smell, so people who smoke it sometimes burn incense to cover up the smell. Joss sticks, special pipes and slang all help to make cannabis seem exotic and mysterious.

Did you know?

More than a third of adult Americans have tried **marijuana**. In 1998 over 700,000 people were arrested. The highest rates of arrest were in Washington, New Jersey and New York. Today the United States spends $27 billion (about £16,875 million) each year trying to prevent drug abuse.

Money well spent?

Do you think governments should spend large sums of money trying to prevent people from taking drugs? How would you dissuade people from taking drugs?

Saying no

What will you do if your friends start to smoke cannabis or if you are offered a **joint**? Many people are worried that if they say no, their friends will think they are stupid and childish. But it is more mature to be able to say you don't want to smoke than to smoke when you don't want to.

Reasons for saying no

This book gives you plenty of reasons for saying no, such as 'It's illegal!' You can think of other possible things that you might say, such as 'I don't want a criminal record' or 'I still have to do my homework'. But you don't have to give an excuse.

You don't need to take cannabis to have fun. These friends are enjoying themselves without smoking or drinking.

What you say matters less than how you say it. If you are sure you don't want to take cannabis, then say so clearly. Friends are more likely to try to persuade you if they sense that you are uncertain. It is perhaps more difficult to say no if you are curious to try cannabis. However, before you consider doing so remember that it is an **illegal drug.**

Life without cannabis

You do not need to smoke cannabis to have a relaxed and enjoyable time with your friends. You can listen to music and talk without getting **stoned** – and you won't be breaking the law.

Working hard at school and doing homework will help you get a better job when you leave school. Smoking cannabis, however, makes some students lose interest in school work.

Dealing with difficult situations

Try to avoid situations in which you might be asked to try cannabis when you do not want to. For example, if you suspect that your friends are going to someone's house to smoke cannabis, it is better to find an excuse not to go, than to go and refuse to join in. If you find yourself in a situation where people are smoking a **joint**, don't panic! If someone is passing round a joint, they are unlikely to mind if you pass it on without trying it.

Finding new friends

If your friends are experimenting with cannabis, alcohol or other things you do not want, you should think about whether they are the best friends for you.

Spending time with your friends and having fun is important, but if they are planning to smoke cannabis or do something you do not want to do, it may be safer to avoid them.

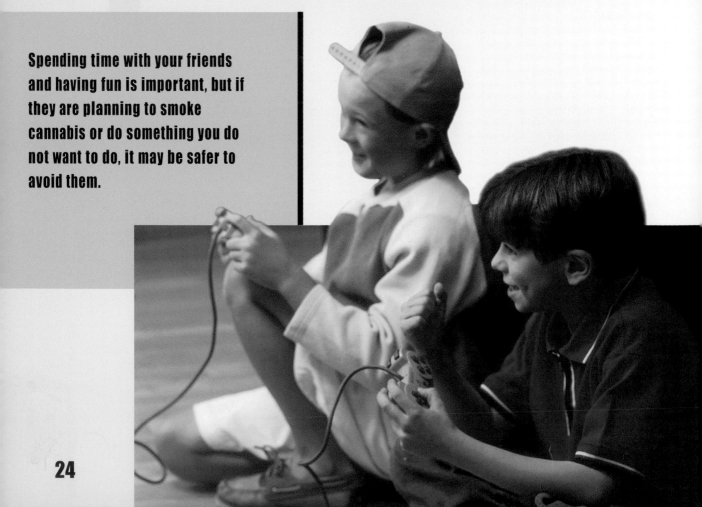

Friendships are important and it is not always easy to change friends. But you can try to spend more time with other people. You could join a club or class at the local sports centre. Exercise not only keeps you fit but makes you feel good. If you are stressed or anxious you will feel more relaxed and calm after doing aerobics or swimming for half an hour, than after smoking a joint.

The pressures of life

Hard work or exams at school and pressure from parents or friends can cause lots of stress. Can cannabis help a person who feels stressed, or would the cannabis just lead to more problems?

Did you know?

Most people who try cannabis do not go on to use it regularly. In Britain it is estimated that up to 6 million people have tried cannabis, but that only a quarter of them still use it.

There are plenty of clubs and activities that you can do after school. You may make new friends this way too.

Growing up

Changing friends

As you grow up, you become more independent of your family. Being in a group with your friends can then seem very important. You might want to be friends with the most exciting people in the class, but it is better to choose friends that you like and who like the same kinds of things as you. Part of growing up is finding out who you are. You may change your group of friends several times as you grow older and discover more about yourself.

The music you listen to and the clothes you like to wear say a lot about who you are. You don't need to smoke cannabis too!

Good and bad times

Growing up is an exciting and enjoyable time. You can try out new things and begin to make decisions for yourself. It can also be a difficult time. There are important exams that you have to work hard for. Friendships with your own sex and the opposite sex won't always run smoothly. Most young people worry about the way they look, whether people will like them, and what they are going to do with their lives.

Getting help

Some young people have serious problems at home or at school. If you have problems that you feel you cannot deal with, don't despair. Ask for help. There are people and organizations who can help you. If you can, ask for help from your family, your friends or your teachers. If at first people don't listen to you, go on looking and asking for help until you get it.

Did you know?

Childline is an organization in Britain that provides help and support for children and young people in trouble or in danger. The number is 0800 1111.

Talking over a problem can help you feel better or help you to find a solution. If you can't talk to a friend or someone in your family, talk to an adult you can trust, such as a teacher.

The cannabis debate

A useful medicine?

Some doctors say that cannabis is a useful **medicine** and should be made legal for certain illnesses and conditions. Sufferers of **multiple sclerosis**, asthma, epilepsy and **AIDS** all find cannabis helpful. People who are taking **chemotherapy** for **cancer** also say that cannabis helps to stop them feeling so ill.

A harmless drug?

Some people think that cannabis should not be an **illegal drug** at all. They say that it is no more harmful than alcohol and much less damaging than smoking tobacco. They think that people should be allowed to make up their own minds about whether or not they use cannabis. People argue that by making cannabis illegal, millions of cannabis-users are being turned into criminals unnecessarily. If the drug was legal, it could be controlled. When someone buys an illegal drug, they have no way of knowing whether it is good quality or whether it has been mixed with tea leaves or something more dangerous, such as **cocaine**.

These people want cannabis to be made legal. They are openly smoking the drug and waiting for the police to arrest them.

Problems of legalizing cannabis

Many people do not want cannabis to be made legal. Three-quarters of Australians, for example, are against it. They say that more people would smoke and not enough is known about its effects on health. Legalizing cannabis would add to existing problems, such as dangerous driving. What do you think?

In Holland the police are quite tolerant of people smoking small amounts of cannabis. This café in Amsterdam sells **joints** as well as coffee and cakes.

Did you know?

Some people want cannabis to be 'decriminalized'. This would mean that it was still illegal to supply, sell or smuggle cannabis but not illegal to have it or smoke it.

Talking point

Rastafarians use cannabis as part of their religion and many ill people use it as a medicine. If the laws on cannabis are strictly applied, many people who do not break any other laws become criminals. Do you think this is fair? If not, what might be a solution to the problem?

Useful contacts

Cannabis

ADFAM National – offers confidential support and information to families and friends of drug users:
telephone: 020 7929 8900.

Australian Drug foundation – for information write to:
409 King Street, Melbourne 3000, Australia
or telephone: 03 9278 8100
or website: www.adf.org.au

Childline – provides free support for children or young people in trouble or danger:
freephone helpline: 0800 1111.

Direct Line – for counselling:
telephone: Australia 1800 136 385

Drugs in School – for advice and support concerning a drug incident in school:
freephone helpline: 0808 8000 800
open Monday-Friday 10.00 am to 5.00 pm.

Drug info Line –
telephone: Victoria 131570 or NSW 02 9361 2111

The National Drugs Helpline – for helpful and friendly advice:
freephone helpline: 0800 77 66 00.

Release – 24-hour confidential helpline offering legal advice concerning arrest on drug charges and other drug matters:
telephone: 020 7603 8654.

Glossary

AIDS a disease which damages the body's ability to fight disease

addictive causing someone to form a habit they cannot give up

cancer a serious illness in which new cells in part of the body grow uncontrollably

caution warning. A legal caution is recorded by the police but does not lead to a charge or a trial.

charged accused by the police

chemotherapy treatment of cancer using strong drugs that poison the cancer

cocaine an illegal drug which is a stimulant

depressant a substance that slows down the body's reactions and relaxes the muscles

diluted made weaker by the addition of water or another liquid

downer a depressant

drug dealing selling drugs

grass a slang name for marijuana

hallucinogen a drug that heightens experiences or makes things which are imagined seem real

hashish brownish-black block made from the whole cannabis plant

hemp the plant family to which cannabis belongs

heroin an addictive, illegal drug made from a particular kind of poppy

illegal drug a drug, such as heroin, LSD or cannabis, which is forbidden by law

joint a cigarette made from cannabis or from cannabis mixed with tobacco

legal drug a substance which affects the body but is allowed by law. Medicines, coffee and tea are legal drugs.

LSD an illegal, powerful hallucinogen

marijuana the dried leaves and stalks of the cannabis plant

medicine substance which is used to treat or cure illnesses

multiple sclerosis disease of the spinal cord and the brain which affects the muscles and causes difficulties with speech

paranoid feeling persecuted without real cause

possession something which is held or owned. A person is said to be in possession of drugs if they hold them or if they can be shown to belong to them.

prematurely too early

prescribed given a medicine under the advice or order of a doctor.

prosecute accuse of a crime and bring to trial

resin a sticky juice that flows from certain plants and trees

sniffer dog a dog trained to smell and search for particular substances, such as drugs

stimulant a substance that speeds up the body

stoned strongly affected by cannabis

tar thick, black sticky substance made by burning tobacco

THC the chemical in cannabis that produces relaxation and hallucinations

upper a stimulant

Index